Project

Science

CW00864548

John Farndon

Miles
Kelly

First published in 2018 by Miles Kelly Publishing Ltd
Harding's Barn, Bardfield End Green, Thaxted, Essex, CM6 3PX, UK

Copyright © Miles Kelly Publishing Ltd 2018

2 4 6 8 10 9 7 5 3 1

Publishing Director Belinda Gallagher
Creative Director Jo Cowan
Senior Editor Amy Johnson
Designers Simon Lee, Andrea Slane
Consultant Ian Graham
Indexer Marie Lorimer
Image Manager Liberty Newton
Production Elizabeth Collins, Jennifer Brunwin-Jones
Reprographics Stephan Davis
Assets Lorraine King

All rights reserved. No part of this publication may be reproduced, stored in a retrieval system, or transmitted by any means, electronic, mechanical, photocopying, recording or otherwise, without the prior permission of the copyright holder.

ISBN 978-1-78617-530-4

Printed in China

British Library Cataloguing-in-Publication Data
A catalogue record for this book is available from the British Library

Made with paper from a sustainable forest

www.mileskelly.net

How to use the projects

IMPORTANT NOTICE
The publisher and author cannot be held responsible for any injuries, damage or loss resulting from the use or misuse of any of the information in this book.

This book is packed full of amazing facts about science. There are also 11 cool projects, designed to make the subject come alive.

Before you start a project:

• Always ask an adult to help you.

• Read the instructions carefully.

• Gather all the supplies you need.

• Clear a surface to work on and cover it with newspaper.

• Wear an apron or old t-shirt to protect your clothing.

Notes for helpers:

• Children will need supervision for the projects, usually because they require the use of scissors, or preparation beforehand.

• Read the instructions together before starting and help to gather the equipment.

SAFETY FIRST!
Be careful when using glue or anything sharp, such as scissors.

How to use
If your project doesn't work the first time, try again — just have fun!

Supplies
The equipment should be easy to find, around the house or from a craft store. Always ask before using materials from home.

Numbered stages
Each stage of the project is numbered and illustrated. Follow the stages in the order shown to complete the project. If glue or paint is used, make sure it is dry before moving onto the next stage.

The big freeze

The temperature at which a substance freezes can vary. In this project you can see how salt affects the freezing point of water.

SUPPLIES
two plastic food tubs • salt • spoon
warm water • marker pen • freezer

WHAT TO DO
1. Fill each tub halfway with warm water.

2. Stir salt into one of the tubs. Keep adding salt until no more will dissolve. Mark the tub that has salt.

3. Put both tubs into the freezer. Check them every two or three hours. What do you notice?

HOW IT WORKS
The tub with salt does not freeze because the salt lowers the water's freezing point.

CONTENTS

ENERGIZE!

Energy is what you need to make things happen. Scientists say it is the ability to perform 'work'. It takes many forms, but you can't either create it or destroy it. When you use energy, you simply swap it to another form.

READY OR HAPPENING?

There are two kinds of energy. Kinetic energy (KE) is energy actually doing something. It is the energy things have when they're moving. Potential energy (PE) is energy that could do something. If you're high up, for instance, you have PE, because gravity can pull you down.

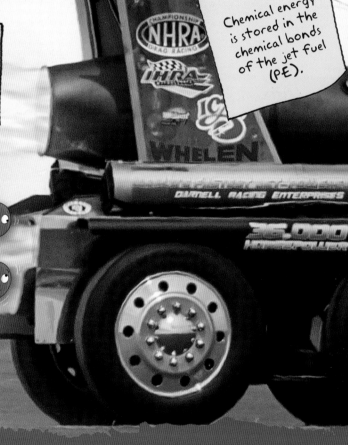

▼ The *Shockwave* jet-powered truck can scorch along at over 600 km/h. Moving this monster so fast involves a LOT of energy.

1 Chemical energy is stored in the chemical bonds of the jet fuel (PE).

2 As the engines burn the fuel, the chemical energy bursts out as heat energy. Heat makes gases swell and generates the thrust that drives the truck forwards.

HEAT AND TEMPERATURE

Heat is the energy of molecules (tiny particles) moving. The faster they move, the hotter things are. Temperature is the way you measure how hot things are. The faster molecules move, the hotter it gets and the higher the temperature.

Extreme degrees

The lowest possible temperature is -273.15°C, which is called **absolute zero**.

The highest temperature known in nature is about **10 billion°C**, in large exploding stars (supernovae).

The lowest temperature recorded on Earth was **-89°C**, in Antarctica.

Energy swing

You can explore the relationship between kinetic energy (KE) and potential energy (PE) with a swing. The idea is to spot when the conversions between KE and PE occur.

WHAT TO DO

1. Sit still on a swing. You currently have stored energy or PE in your muscles.

2. Now push off with your leg muscles and move your body to help you swing higher. You are converting the PE of your muscles into the KE of movement.

3. By moving your body, you can gain enough momentum to swing high. As you swing up, the KE turns into PE – the energy gravity gives because of your height.

4. At the highest point of your swing, you run out of KE and can go no higher. But you have built up a lot of PE.

5. As you swing back down again and pick up speed, the PE is converted to KE. The KE will carry you right back up the other side and you will build up PE again.

3

As the truck accelerates, the heat energy changes to KE.

The highest temperature recorded on Earth was 56.7°C, in Death Valley, USA.

WHERE DO WE GET ENERGY?

We get most of the energy we need to carry on our lives from burning coal, oil and gas. These are called fossil fuels because they are made from remains of living things. But burning fossil fuels causes pollution – and supplies will eventually run out. So more people are using cleaner renewable energy such as wind and solar energy.

FORCE AND MOTION

A force is a push or pull. It changes the speed, direction or shape of something. Objects have natural inertia — they only move when forced. Once moving, they have momentum, meaning they move at the same speed and direction until forced to change.

MOTION RULES!

In the 1600s, the great scientist Sir Isaac Newton came up with three rules about force and movement, known as the Laws of Motion:

1. Things only accelerate or decelerate when forced to.
2. The acceleration depends on how strong the force is and how great the mass being accelerated is.
3. Every force or action is balanced by an equal force in the opposite direction.

FIRST LAW

Booster rockets provide the force needed to launch a space rocket from the ground. Once it reaches the right speed the boosters can be jettisoned.

THIRD LAW

A rocket can move through empty space even though it seems to have nothing to push against. As burning gases swell out from the engines, they push against the rocket. So the rocket is pushed forward just as much as the gases are pushed back.

GETTING THE GS

Extreme accelerations are sometimes measured in 'g's – that is, how they compare to the acceleration when you fall due to gravity. A top-fuel dragster can accelerate from zero to 160 km/h in 0.86 seconds. That is a horizontal acceleration of 5.3 g – 5.3 times faster than you fall!

SECOND LAW

Space scientists can use Newton's law to work out just how much rocket power they will need to lift (accelerate) a certain weight, or payload.

▲ To get a spacecraft into space, it has to get moving fast enough to overcome Earth's gravity.

Reaction rocket

A rocket is propelled by the action and reaction between the rocket body and the fuel. In the same way, this water rocket is propelled by the reaction force between the water and the air you pump in to the bottle. Make sure an adult helps you with this project.

SUPPLIES

plastic soft drinks bottle • cork that fits snugly into the mouth of the bottle • long thin screw and screwdriver
bicycle pump plus needle adaptor for inflating balls
strong glue or adhesive tape • thick card • scissors

HOW TO MAKE

1. Using the screw, carefully make a hole in the cork that fits the needle adaptor snugly, and push the adaptor in – it needs to go all the way through.

2. Cut out three fins from the card. Stick them securely to the top of the bottle using the glue or tape.

3. Quarter-fill the bottle with water, insert the cork and connect the pump.

4. Take your rocket to an open space and stand it upside down on the fins.

5. Keeping your face clear, pump air in. Pressure will build up until your rocket blasts off!

PULLING TOGETHER

When you drop something, it doesn't just fall of its own accord. It falls because it's pulled towards Earth by a force called gravity. Gravity is what keeps us on the ground, and why the planets go round the Sun.

Orbits balance momentum and gravity. The Moon's momentum alone would send it hurtling into space, but the pull of Earth's gravity tugs it into a circle around Earth.

Moon

Earth

UNIVERSAL ATTRACTION

Gravity is the mutual force of attraction that holds the Universe together. Every bit of matter in the Universe has its own gravity pull and attracts everything else. The strength of the pull depends on how massive things are and how far apart. Objects with more mass pull more strongly than those with less.

◀ In space, things go round each other in paths called orbits. The planets in our Solar System, as well as other objects such as asteroids and comets, all orbit the Sun because it has a massive pull of gravity.

Parachute power

If there was no air, a feather would fall at the same speed as a lead weight. But air slows things down, as you can see with this simple parachute.

SUPPLIES

plastic carrier bag • ruler • pencil scissors • thin string • two small plastic toys, roughly the same size adhesive tape

HOW TO MAKE

1. Cut a 10 cm square from the bag. Using the scissors, make a tiny hole in each corner.

2. Thread a piece of string through each hole and tie it in place.

3. Tie or stick all four strings to one of the toys.

HOW TO USE

Find a place indoors from where you can drop the toys. Drop the toy with the parachute and the other toy at the same time. Which one reaches the ground first?

HOW IT WORKS

The toy with the parachute takes longer to reach the ground because the parachute's large area means it hits a lot of air as it falls, slowing it down.

HEAVY!

When something is heavy, you might talk of its weight. But scientists talk only of mass. Mass is how much matter there is. For scientists, weight is a force; it's how strongly gravity pulls. Weight is measured as a force in units called newtons, whereas pounds and kilograms are measures of mass. So weightlifters should be called masslifters!

TOP OF THE WORLD

In 2012, daredevil skydiver Felix Baumgartner jumped from a capsule 39 km above the ground. When he first started to fall, he accelerated rapidly, reaching 1357.64 km/h. The force of the air pushing on him (air resistance) increased as he gained speed. Eventually the air resistance became equal to his weight, and he then fell steadily at the same speed, called terminal velocity.

◀ Jumping from the top of the stratosphere, it took just over 9 minutes for Baumgartner to reach the ground.

PUSHING IT

Pressure is the amount of force acting over an area. Air and water exert pressure as they are always pushing against their surroundings. This is the combined effect of the molecules in water and air constantly moving, whizzing around at speeds of 1500 km/h or more.

Pressure planet

The planet Venus has such a thick atmosphere that its pressure is **90 times** that of Earth's.

Robot vehicles may be sent to land on Venus in the future.

Venus rovers will need to be built **super strong** to avoid being quickly crushed.

UNDER PRESSURE

When you squeeze water or air molecules into a smaller space, the molecules jostle harder and the pressure rises. Similarly, adding heat increases pressure as the molecules zoom about faster and smash into things more forcefully. In a geyser, underground water is superheated and squeezed into very small spaces, creating great pressure.

▶ Geysers are found near active volcanic areas where there is magma (molten rock) underground. The magma superheats the water, creating enough pressure to shoot out a scalding jet at the surface.

Bottle crusher

We are so used to air pressure that it's hard to imagine its power. But you can witness it for yourself in this simple experiment with steam in a bottle. It's crushing!

SUPPLIES

plastic soft drinks bottle with a screw top • a little hot water cold or iced water

WHAT TO DO

1. Ask an adult to quarter-fill the bottle with really hot water from a tap or kettle.

2. Leave to stand for a few seconds, then screw the lid on tight.

3. Hold the bottle under a running cold tap, or place in a bowl of iced water. The bottle will instantly be crushed.

HOW IT WORKS

As the cold water chills the hot air inside the bottle, the air shrinks. The pressure of the air outside instantly crushes the bottle.

KEY

1. Groundwater seeps down through tiny channels in the rock. The water comes from rain, snow and often nearby rivers and lakes.

2. The pressure increases as the water travels further below the surface.

3. Heat from the magma chamber heats the water. Under such pressure, water reaches very high temperatures but does not boil — this is called superheating.

4. The water rises rapidly, forced through a kind of underground plumbing system of narrow channels and cracks in the rock.

5. Water and steam collect in chambers. The steam bubbles out slowly, heating the water above. The water boils suddenly, releasing pressure and spewing out water and steam.

6. In a hot spring, rising water is cooled by groundwater before reaching the surface. The pressure drops, so the water flows out steadily rather than erupting.

DRIVING WINDS

Weather forecasters monitor variations in pressure in the air closely, because pressure variations are what makes our weather and drives all winds. When the air gets cold in one place and sinks, the pressure increases. That pushes air towards low pressure areas where the air is warmer and rising.

▶ In this satellite image, clouds reveal the spiral pattern of winds circulating a low pressure zone.

11

FLOATING AND FLYING

It's amazing that heavy aeroplanes can fly, and big ships can float. After all, even a tiny stone will fall through the air and sink in water. But both planes and ships use their shape to maximize the support given by molecules, which give lift in air and buoyancy in water.

ON THE SURFACE

When an object is submerged in water, it's pulled down by its weight. But the water pushes back up with a buoyancy force equal to the weight of water displaced (pushed out of the way) by the object. If the object is less dense than water, it floats. It is said to be buoyant.

1 Boat displaces a certain volume of water

2 Displaced water causes a buoyancy force

3 When the weight of the displaced water equals the weight of the boat, the boat floats

▲ A heavy metal ship can float because its large hull pushes enough water out of the way to create a huge upthrust, enough to keep it afloat. The key is the air trapped inside the hull, which reduces the ship's overall density.

FLOATING ON AIR

Just as ships can float on water, so balloons can float on air. Here the balloon must be filled with a gas that is less dense than air. That way the balloon becomes naturally buoyant and rises through the air, just like a cork bobs up through water. The gas in the balloon could be helium, which is lighter than air, or hot air, which is lighter than cool air.

◄ Burners add more hot air whenever the balloon needs to climb.

Wing lifted

2 Above the wing, the air spreads around the curved surface, creating low pressure

▼ If you look at a plane wing side-on, you can see the aerofoil shape. It has a curved topside and a flat or curved underside.

Leading edge

4 The difference in pressure causes the air to accelerate downwards behind the wing. This causes the wing to lift

1 The flow of air is diverted over and under the wing

3 Below the wing there is an area of high air pressure

Downward force on air

GIVING A LIFT

The wings of a plane have a special downcurve and slice through the air at an angle, a shape known as an aerofoil. This diverts the flow of air over and under the wings in a special way and alters how the air pushes on the wing. It pushes less on top of the wing and more from beneath, and so the wing is lifted.

The **wandering albatross** has the longest wings of any bird, up to 3.5 m across. They help give it enough **lift** to glide for hours at a time.

Sink or float!

See how shape can give a boat buoyancy by reshaping a ball of modelling clay into a boat that floats.

SUPPLIES
modelling clay • basin or large bowl of cold water

WHAT TO DO
1. Lower a large ball of modelling clay into the water.

2. You will see that the ball sinks – this is because it is denser than water. The water level rises because water is displaced by the ball as it sinks.

3. Take the ball out and reshape it to make a bowl-shaped boat with tall sides.

4. Place the clay back in the water. This time it should float, even though it has the same weight. This is because the shape displaces a larger volume of water, due to the air it contains.

THE LITTLEST THINGS

All matter is built up from tiny pieces called atoms. Atoms are so minuscule two billion could fit on this full stop. Scientists once thought atoms were the smallest things of all, but it was then discovered that they are actually more like clouds — mostly empty space, dotted with even tinier 'sub-atomic particles'.

INSIDE AN ATOM

At the core of every atom is its nucleus, a cluster of two kinds of particle: protons and neutrons. Even tinier particles, electrons, whizz around the nucleus. But don't imagine sub-atomic particles as tiny solid balls; they are just concentrations of energy that occur in particular places.

Nucleus

Oxygen atom

Carbon atom

Oxygen atom

▶ A molecule is made up of two or more atoms chemically bonded together. In this carbon dioxide molecule, a carbon atom is bonded to two oxygen atoms.

▲ The number of electrons in an atom always matches the number of protons, so an atom has a neutral electrical charge. There are eight protons and eight electrons in this oxygen atom.

FOUR FORCES

Atoms can be split, but they are usually held together by three forces – the electrical attraction between the negative electrons and positive protons and the 'strong' and 'weak' forces that bind the particles of the nucleus together. These three forces, together with gravity, are the basic forces of nature that hold the entire Universe together.

Quark

Electrons have a negative electrical charge

▲ A proton composed of three quarks. Quarks are a very important type of particle, as they combine to make up protons and neutrons.

▶ The nucleus of an oxygen atom.

Scientists now have **microscopes** powerful enough to actually see **atoms**.

Proton

Neutron

Protons have a positive electrical charge; neutrons have none

The tiniest of all

By smashing atoms together at high speeds, scientists have discovered 200 different sub-atomic particles. They're all made from two kinds: quarks and leptons. Electrons are leptons. Protons and neutrons are built up from quarks. There are six 'flavours' of quarks, and scientists have given them strange names.

Up quark

Down quark

Top quark

Bottom quark

Charm quark

Strange quark

WHAT'S THE MATTER?

Every substance in the Universe — everything that's not just empty space — consists of matter. It has three main forms — solid, liquid and gas. These are called the states of matter. They seem different, but they can switch from one to the other and back if the temperature and pressure is right.

A gas does not have any shape or strength, and swells to fill any space. This is because the molecules move so fast that they do not hold together.

A solid has a definite shape. This is because its molecules are tightly packed and locked together in a regular structure and just vibrate on the spot. The hotter it gets, the more they vibrate.

A liquid flows and spreads out to take the shape of any container it is poured into. This is because the bonds between the molecules are loose enough to slide over each other like dry sand.

MOLECULES AND MATTER

Every substance is made of molecules. It's the way the molecules interact that makes it solid, liquid or gas. Water is one of the few substances that naturally occurs in all three states – solid as ice, liquid as water, and as a gas called water vapour. Liquid water can also be changed into a hot gas called steam by heating it until it boils.

▲ Uniquely, water expands when it freezes, so ice is less dense than water. This is why icebergs just about float.

SWITCHING STATES

As a substance warms up, its molecules move more and more. So it goes from solid to liquid (melting) and from liquid to gas (evaporation). As a substance cools down, the molecules move less and less. So they go from gas to liquid (condensing) and from liquid to solid (freezing).

▲ Gallium is a metal with a melting point of 29.8°C. This is low enough that it would melt in the palm of your hand.

PLASMA

Plasma is a fourth state of matter. It occurs when a gas gets so hot and the molecules become so energetic that they release tiny electrical charges. This makes the gas ionized (electrically charged).

▶ In a plasma ball, glowing loops of plasma are created by a high voltage current surging through a noble gas.

Points of change

Water boils at 100°C and freezes at 0°C.

Helium has the lowest freezing point of any substance at −272.2°C.

Tungsten has the highest melting point of any metal at 3422°C.

Carbon has the highest melting point of any substance at over 4000°C.

The big freeze

The temperature at which a substance freezes can vary. In this project you can see how salt affects the freezing point of water.

SUPPLIES

two plastic food tubs • salt • spoon warm water • marker pen • freezer

WHAT TO DO

1. Fill each tub halfway with warm water.

2. Stir salt into one of the tubs. Keep adding salt until no more will dissolve. Mark the tub that has salt.

3. Put both tubs into the freezer. Check them every two or three hours. What do you notice?

HOW IT WORKS

The tub with salt does not freeze because the salt lowers the water's freezing point.

GETTING A REACTION

When you see a candle burn, metal go rusty or a cake rise in the oven, you are seeing a chemical reaction. This is when different chemicals meet and react, changing each other to form new chemicals. Some reactions are slow and gentle, but some explosive.

BURNING BRIGHT

Burning is a chemical reaction called combustion. When things burn, heat makes one substance, known as a fuel, combine chemically with oxygen. This makes a whole lot more heat. The fuel can be a solid, such as coal, a liquid like oil, or a gas such as natural gas. The oxygen usually comes from the air.

GOING RUSTY

Rusting, like burning, is a reaction involving oxygen. This time, though, it is a slow reaction in which iron slowly disintegrates as it reacts with water and oxygen, forming a brown crust of hydrated iron oxide. Salt water speeds this up.

▶ The nails exposed to water and oxygen (far left) and salt water and oxygen (far right) have rusted. Those in the middle have not, as they are missing water (left) or oxygen (right).

Make an explosion!

You can see for yourself the power of a reaction with this simple experiment. Make sure you do this with an adult watching.

SUPPLIES

tube of Mentos • one large bottle of diet fizzy drink goggles • sheet of A4 paper • large open space

WHAT TO DO

1. Go out into an open space, open the bottle and stand it on the ground.

2. Roll the paper into a simple funnel shape and place 4-6 Mentos inside.

3. Hold the funnel over the opening of the bottle and let the Mentos fall in. Now run!

HOW IT WORKS

It was once thought this explosion was a chemical reaction. But scientists now think that it is caused by microscopic pits in the surface of the Mentos. The pits encourage carbon dioxide dissolved in the fizzy drink to form gas bubbles, so it is actually a physical reaction.

▼ Fireworks blaze in different colours because they contain traces of chemicals such as lithium (which burns red), calcium (which burns orange) and copper (which burns blue).

▶ When nitric acid reacts with copper, it creates brown nitrogen dioxide gas and bright green copper nitrate solution.

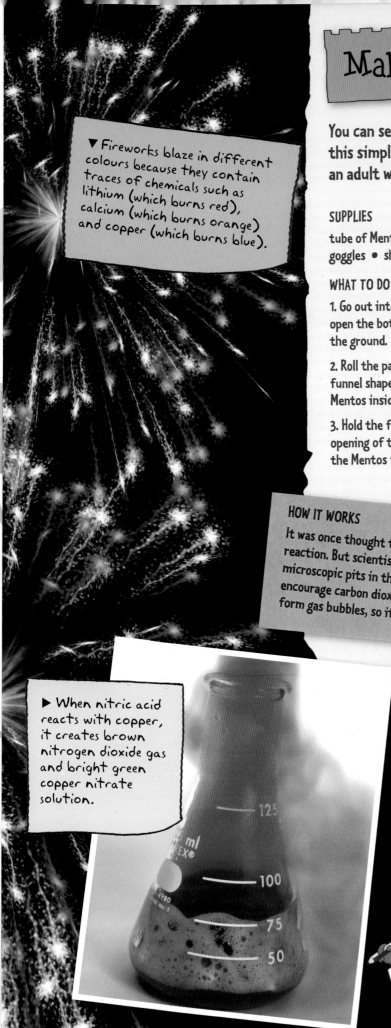

DRAMATIC ACIDS

Strong acids are extremely dangerous because they react so powerfully. Acids contain hydrogen. When mixed with water, the hydrogen atoms are turned loose as reactive particles called ions. Acids can cause terrible skin burns. For example, sulphuric acid absorbs water in a reaction that creates heat. Strong acids also dissolve metals.

MAGNETIZE!

Magnetism is the invisible force of attraction or repulsion between magnetic materials such as iron. Each magnet has an area around it in which it exerts its force, called its magnetic field. The field gets weaker further from the magnet.

THE POWER OF POLES

Magnetic force is especially strong at the ends of a magnet – the poles. One is called the north pole because if the magnet is suspended freely it swings to point north. The other is the south pole. If opposite poles come together, they attract; if like poles come together, they repel.

▼ Maglev trains have no wheels but float along the track electromagnetically.

▼ Electromagnets in the train and guideway (track) generate a magnetic force that keeps them slightly apart. So the train is held above the track without touching it.

Train

Guideway

Undercarriage of train

ELECTRIC MAGNETS

Electricity and magnetism are deeply linked. Every electric current creates a magnetic field around it, and moving a magnet past an electric wire generates a current in it. An electromagnet is a coil of wire with an iron core that becomes a strong magnet when the current is switched on. This is the basis for super-fast trains called maglevs (magnetic levitation), which run without any wheels.

Make a compass

A compass is a device that uses a magnet to show the direction of Earth's North Pole. Here you can learn how to make your own!

SUPPLIES

bar magnet • large sewing needle • plastic bowl • cork coaster

HOW TO MAKE

1. Magnetize the needle by stroking it with the magnet 20 times in the same direction. Do this in a looping motion, lifting the magnet away between each stroke.

2. Half-fill the bowl with water, then carefully float the cork coaster as near to the centre as possible.

3. Lay the magnetized needle carefully on the cork, as close to the centre as you can. This makes a simple compass, and the needle should turn to point north.

SKY LIGHTS

Sometimes the sky near Earth's poles is filled with glowing lights called aurorae. These are created by charged particles streaming from the Sun. They are pulled into Earth's magnetic field near the poles, where they collide with atoms in the atmosphere. These collisions make bursts of light energy.

▶ Aurorae appear in the sky as dancing curtains of brilliantly coloured light.

◀ The influence of Earth's magnetic field stretches far out into space, a region called the magnetosphere.

LIGHTEN UP

We see things by light. It is radiation emitted by atoms, coming from sources such as the Sun, other stars and electric lights. There are other kinds of radiation, but only light is visible. It always travels in straight lines so people talk about light rays, but rays are really the path light takes.

▼ A glass wedge or prism bends normal white light so that it splits apart to reveal all the colours it contains. This rainbow is called a spectrum.

Prism

White light

WHAT IS LIGHT?

It is best to think of light as vibrating packets of energy. Light energy is emitted as tiny particles called photons. A beam of light is made of millions of photons. The colour varies according to the wavelength, or the vibration pattern, of the photons.

RAINBOW COLOURS

All the colours in a rainbow are different wavelengths of light. Mixed together, the colours blend into white light, which is what the light from the Sun is. But you can split them apart by refracting them (bending at an angle) through a prism to create a spectrum, or through raindrops to create a rainbow.

▼ Each colour is made by light with a different wavelength. The longest waves are red, the shortest are violet.

FAST AS LIGHT

Light is the fastest thing in the Universe. In space, it travels at 299,792,458 m/s, and can travel from the Sun to the Earth in 8 minutes. It travels slightly slower in air, and slower still in water.

Red   Orange   Yellow   Green   Blue

REFLECTION OR REFRACTION?

When light rays hit a surface, some bounce off. This is reflection. Very smooth surfaces act as mirrors, reflecting almost all of the light that hits them (1). If the surface is transparent, like glass, some will pass through (2). If light rays strike a surface at an angle, they may be refracted (3). This is because they change speed when they pass from one substance to another, such as from air to glass.

Spectrum

Build a periscope

Light travels in straight lines – but mirrors can make it change direction. You can see this for yourself by making a simple periscope to let you see round corners!

SUPPLIES

cereal box • two small square mirrors • masking tape • glue ruler • pencil • scissors paints and paintbrush

HOW TO MAKE

1. Cut the cereal box so you're left with only the front or back. Copy the template onto the inside. The four columns should each be the same width as the mirrors. The flaps at the ends need to be the same size as the mirrors – measure to make sure.

2. Cut out the template along the solid lines. Using the scissors and ruler, carefully score along all the dotted lines.

3. Fold along each scored line and bend into a box shape. Put glue on the tabs and stick the tabs to the sides. Secure with masking tape if needed. Stick down the flaps.

4. Put glue on the backs of the mirrors and stick one in each of the openings.

5. Paint your periscope. Once it's dry, you can use it to look over walls and round corners!

Make sure these flaps are the same size as the mirrors

Tabs

1

Tab

Score and fold the dotted lines

Tabs

Cut along the solid lines

2

3

4

5

SOUNDING OUT

When anything makes a sound, it sends out vibrations, or sound waves, that squeeze then stretch the air (or water). Sound waves cannot travel through a vacuum such as space because there is nothing to transmit them.

ECHOLOCATION

To locate things in the dark or underwater, creatures such as bats and dolphins emit high-pitched squeaks. When the sound hits something, it bounces back as an echo. From the echo, the animal can tell where the object is, as well as its size and shape.

MEASURING SOUND

If sound waves are frequent, the sound they make is high-pitched. Loud sounds are made when the waves are high energy. The loudness of sound is measured in decibels (dB). An increase of 10 dB doubles the loudness of the sound you hear.

dB

leaves rustling		passing car			
0	10	20	30	40	50	60	70	80	90	100	110	120	130
	pin dropping		whisper			normal conversation			hairdryer			rock concert	firewo

► A supersonic jet plane flies faster than sound. Its speed is described in Mach numbers - the speed of the plane relative to the speed of sound locally. When a plane flies faster than sound, it often creates a 'sonic boom' - a loud bang caused by the sudden squeezing of air.

The cloud of vapour shown here is a shockwave created as the plane approaches supersonic speed

THE SPEED OF SOUND

Sound takes time to travel. That's why you often see a flash of lightning before you hear the rumble of thunder it sets off. On average, it travels at 340 m/s in air, and slightly faster in warm air. In water, it travels much further and up to four times faster. In solids such as metals, it travels faster still.

Water music

Learn about pitch and make music at the same time!

SUPPLIES

six strong tall drinking glasses or identical glass bottles water • thick chopstick • piano or keyboard (online will do)

WHAT TO DO

1. Fill each glass with a different amount of water. Try to make the differences fairly even.

2. Tap each glass gently with the chopstick. Do they make different-pitched sounds? Which glass makes the highest sound and which the lowest?

3. You will see that the less water there is in the glass, the higher the note (higher pitch). Try adding a little water to the glass or taking it away until they match the pitch of keys on the piano.

4. You now have your own water xylophone. Play some music!

HOW IT WORKS

The glass passes on the vibrations of the stick hitting it to the water. The shorter the column of water, the higher the pitch as the sound waves are higher frequency. So the glass with the most water produces the lowest sound.

INDEX

Page numbers in **bold** refer to main subjects.

A
absolute zero 4
acceleration 5, **6**, **7**, 9
acids 18, **23**
aerofoils **13**
air pressure 10, **11**
air resistance 9
atoms **14–15**, **16**, 19, 23, 24, 27, 28
aurorae **27**

B, C
batteries 24, 25
buoyancy **12**, 13
chemical reactions **22–23**
combustion **22**, 23
compass 27
compounds **19**

D
decibels 30
drag 13

E
echolocation **30**
electricity 15, 16, 21, **24–25**, 26
electromagnets **26**
electrons 14, 15, 24, 25
elements **16–19**
energy **4–5**, 14, 27, 28
explosions 23

F
fireworks **22–23**
floating **12**, 20
flying **13**
forces 6, 7, 9, 10, 12, **13**, **15**, 26
freezing 20, 21

G
gases **20**, 21, 22
geothermal energy 5
geysers 10
gravity 4, 5, 7, **8–9**, 13, 15

H
heat energy **4**, 5
hydroelectricity 5

K, L
kinetic energy (KE) **4**, 5
Laws of Motion **6–7**
leptons 15
lift **13**
light energy 27, **28–29**
lightning 25, 31
liquids **20**, 21, 22

M
magnetic fields 26, 27
magnetism **26–27**
magnetosphere 27
mass 8, **9**
matter 8, 14, **20–21**
metals 16, 19, 21, 23, 31
molecules 4, 10, 11, **14**, 19, **20**, 21
momentum 5, 6, 8
motion **6–7**

N, O
neutrons 14, 15
noble gases 16, 19
orbits 8

P, Q
Periodic Table **16–19**
periscopes 29
photons 28

pitch 30, 31
planes 12, 13, 31
plasma **21**
potential energy (PE) **4**, 5
protons 14, 15, 16, 24
quarks 15

R
radiation **28**
rainbows 28
rare earths 19
reflection **29**
refraction 28, **29**
renewable energy **5**
rockets 6–7
rust **22**

S
solar energy 5
solids **20**, 21, 22
sonic boom 31
sound **30–31**
sound waves **30**, 31
spectrum 28
speed of light **28**
speed of sound **31**
static electricity **24**, 25
sub-atomic particles **14**, **15**

T
temperature **4**, 21
terminal velocity 9
thrust 13

W
water pressure **10**, 11
weather systems 10, 11
white light 28

ACKNOWLEDGEMENTS

The publishers would like to thank the following artists who have contributed to this book:

Cover Paul Boston (Meiklejohn Illustration)

Insides Sara Lynn Cramb (Astound) and Tom Heard (The Bright Agency)

All other artwork is from the Miles Kelly Artwork Bank

The publishers would like to thank the following sources for the use of their photographs:

t = top, c = centre, b = bottom, l = left, r = right, m = main

Alamy 23(bl) E. R. Degginger; 26(m) Bernd Mellmann

NASA 8–9(m) NASA/JPL; 21(cr, under flap) ESA/NASA/SOHO
Rex Features 9(br) Red Bull Content Pool/REX/Shutterstock
Science Photo Library 6–7(m) David Ducros, ESA; 11(b) University of Dundee; 14–15(m) Mikkel Juul Jensen; 19(tr) Alexandre Dotta; 22(br) Andrew Lambert Photography
Shutterstock.com 4–5(m) Santiparp Wattanaporn; 9(bl) Ana del Castillo; 12(bl) XAOC; 14(bl) Orange Deer; 19(br) EpicStockMedia; 20(m) Sergey Nivens; 21(tl) e_rik, (cr) Nikolay Petkov; 25(t) kornilov007; 27(cr) John A Davis; 28–29(m) XYZ; 31(t) Anatoliy Lukich

Every effort has been made to acknowledge the source and copyright holder of each picture. Miles Kelly Publishing apologizes for any unintentional errors or omissions.